ANIMAL SURVIVAL

FLEEING TO SURVIVE

BY LAURA PERDEW

CONTENT CONSULTANT
KATHRYN E. SPILIOS, PhD
DEPARTMENT OF BIOLOGY
BOSTON UNIVERSITY

Kids Core

An Imprint of Abdo Publishing
abdobooks.com

abdobooks.com

Published by Abdo Publishing, a division of ABDO, PO Box 398166, Minneapolis, Minnesota 55439. Copyright © 2023 by Abdo Consulting Group, Inc. International copyrights reserved in all countries. No part of this book may be reproduced in any form without written permission from the publisher. Kids Core™ is a trademark and logo of Abdo Publishing.

Printed in the United States of America, North Mankato, Minnesota.
052022
092022

Cover Photo: Volodymyr Burdiak/Shutterstock Images
Interior Photos: Zoltan Tarlacz/Shutterstock Images, 4–5; Andrea Izzotti/Shutterstock Images, 7, 28 (top); Vlada Cech/Shutterstock Images, 8; Mogens Trolle/Shutterstock Images, 10–11, 28 (bottom); Shutterstock Images, 12, 14, 16–17, 25 (passive wing), 25 (hovering wing), 26, 29 (top); Jennifer White Maxwell/Shutterstock Images, 18; Bence Mate/Nature Picture Library/Alamy, 20; Photoshot/Avalon Red/Alamy, 22–23, 29 (bottom); Vladimir Strnad/Shutterstock Images, 25 (active wing); Nick Vorobey/Shutterstock Images, 25 (elliptical wing); Jamil Bin Mat Isa/Shutterstock Images, 25 (high-speed wing)

Editor: Ann Schwab
Series Designer: Katharine Hale

Library of Congress Control Number: 2021951723

Publisher's Cataloging-in-Publication Data

Names: Perdew, Laura, author.
Title: Fleeing to survive / by Laura Perdew
Description: Minneapolis, Minnesota : Abdo Publishing, 2023 | Series: Animal survival | Includes online resources and index.
Identifiers: ISBN 9781532198496 (lib. bdg.) | ISBN 9781644947661 (pbk.) | ISBN 9781098272142 (ebook)
Subjects: LCSH: Animal defenses--Juvenile literature. | Defense measures--Juvenile literature. | Adaptation (Physiology)--Juvenile literature. | Animal behavior--Juvenile literature.
Classification: DDC 591.57--dc23

CONTENTS

Prairie dogs hover near their burrows, on high alert for a predator.

CHAPTER 1

ESCAPE!

A colony of prairie dogs grazes. One watches for predators. It spots a coyote! It sounds the alarm. *Yip!*

The call warns the others. All the prairie dogs scramble toward the entrances to their **burrows**. But they don't go in yet.

The coyote gets closer. The prairie dogs stay alert. When the coyote is too close, the prairie dog on watch yips again. They all flee into burrows. In their underground homes, they are safe. The coyote will have to look somewhere else for a meal.

Fleeing

Animals flee from danger in many ways. Some run, hop, or jump. Other animals swim, slide,

Other Dangers

Predators are not the only danger animals face. Storms are also a threat. These include hurricanes, tornadoes, blizzards, and floods. Animals must be aware of wildfires too. In each case, animals determine the risk. They flee to safety if needed.

A kangaroo hops away from a bushfire in Australia.

or slither. They might fly or glide. Or they creep and crawl. Many animals flee in flocks, **schools**, or herds. Some animals flee to safe hiding places. Others simply outrun their predators.

A wolf chasing prey can run up to 35 miles per hour (56 km/h).

Animals don't always flee right away. Like the prairie dogs, many wait. They watch the predator and consider the risk. Animals do this to save their energy. They also may not want to miss an opportunity to eat.

An animal's **escape response** depends on the situation. Each animal reacts differently. And it depends whether they flee on land, in the air, or in the water.

Sir David Attenborough narrates the documentary *The Hunt: Part I.* He describes a scene where wolves are hunting a hare:

> A hare can change direction in an instant. If it can continue to sidestep and **jink**, it may ultimately outlast [the wolves].

Source: "Best Scenes from *The Hunt*—Part 1." *YouTube*, uploaded by BBC Earth, 9 May 2020, youtube.com. Accessed 23 Nov. 2021.

Comparing Texts

Think about the quote. Does it support the information in this chapter? Or does it give a different perspective? Explain how in a few sentences.

Zebras try to change directions to confuse the lion pursuing them.

CHAPTER 2

SEEKING SAFETY ON LAND

On land, animals flee to safety in many different ways. But they don't always move at full speed. Moving quickly takes a lot of energy. Some move at an angle so they can keep an eye on the predator. Others flee in a zigzag line or loop around.

Fleeing to a hiding place can help a snake stay safe.

Some twist and turn. These escape responses make the prey harder to catch.

Run, Slither, and Hop

Researchers studying zebras found that lower-speed chases were the animals' best chance for survival. Moving at a slower speed allows the animals to make sudden turns at the last moment. This confuses their predators. It gives the animals a chance to escape.

Most snakes rely on **camouflage** to stay safe. But if that doesn't work, their best defense is a quick slither under rocks or into burrows. Or they can slither into a tree or bush.

Losing a Body Part

Some animals lose a body part to escape danger. Many lizards will shed their tails. Crabs can shed a claw. A daddy longlegs spider can lose a leg. Often, the separated body part will keep moving. The flopping and twitching distract the predator. Luckily, many of these animals will grow the body part back!

Most frogs can jump 20 times their body length!

Some land animals jump and hop to get away from danger. Frogs, crickets, and rabbits are excellent leapers. In the desert, kangaroo rats rely on their speed and athletic ability. Their powerful back legs allow them to jump nearly 9 feet (2.75 m) at a time. They can escape a predator in one leap!

Further Evidence

Look at the website below. Does it give any new evidence to support Chapter Two?

How a Frog Jumps

abdocorelibrary.com/fleeing-to -survive

Capybaras, the largest living rodents, use water to escape predators.

CHAPTER 3

WATER RESCUE

Not all land animals flee on land. Some escape into the water. Capybaras, found in Central and South America, dive into water to escape danger. They can stay underwater for up to five minutes.

Fire ants can float on top of the water by clinging together to form a raft.

Water Escapes

When a flood threatens a nest of fire ants, they flee as a group. The ants clump together on the surface of the water. Then they flatten out to create a raft. They can float like that for weeks until the water dries up.

Many fish swim in schools. Often, these schools quickly change direction in the water. This confuses their predators. Other fish simply use speed to escape danger.

Escape Hatching

Red-eyed tree frogs lay their eggs at the edge of ponds. Many of the eggs are eaten by snakes. But not all. Tadpoles that have developed in eggs for at least five days can hatch early to flee. If they sense danger, escape hatching might help them survive.

The basilisk lizard can evade predators by running on water.

The basilisk lizard of Central America flees on top of the water! When threatened, it drops to the water. Then, it runs across the surface to escape. It may also dive. It can stay underwater for ten minutes.

Experts at the American Museum of Natural History explain how a basilisk lizard runs on water:

> The long toes of the hind feet are fringed with scales that spread out as the foot strikes the water . . . They churn their legs . . . creating pockets of air with their big, fringed feet.

Source: "Green Basilisk." *American Museum of Natural History*, n.d., amnh.org. Accessed 23 Nov. 2021.

What's the Big Idea?

Read this quote carefully. What is its main idea? Explain how the main idea is supported by details.

Flying squirrels glide from tree to tree using the skin stretched between their front and back legs as a parachute.

CHAPTER 4

FLYING FROM DANGER

Some animals, like the flying squirrel, take to the air to flee. These squirrels have a **membrane** between their front and back legs. When they spread their limbs, the membrane works like a parachute. They can glide from tree to tree.

Flying snakes and flying frogs are great gliders too. Flying fish can jump out of the water. They can glide through the air more than 655 feet (200 m). Putting multiple glides together, they can cover up to 1,312 feet (400 m) at once.

True Flyers

Birds, insects, and bats are adapted to true flight. Most birds are expert flyers. They have feathers and hollow, lightweight bones. Their wings are perfectly shaped for catching air. When in danger, most birds can fly to safety.

Lift Off! Bird Wings and Flight

Active Soaring Wings
These long, narrow wings are excellent for soaring over water when wind currents are steady.

Passive Soaring Wings
These long, broad wings have gaps at the ends of the feathers to help the bird use rising hot air to soar.

Elliptical Wings
These wings are best for quick take-offs, flying by tree branches, and avoiding predators.

High-Speed Wings
These medium-to-long, narrow wings are used for long-range flying.

Hovering Wings
These small wings are used for hovering and focused flight.

The size and shape of a bird's wings affect how it can fly. This chart shows how the different types of wings are used.

Dragonflies have two sets of strong, flexible wings that can work independently of each other.

Most insects have two sets of wings. Dragonflies are master flyers. They can fly in any direction, hover, and move quickly.

Eye of the Hurricane

A hurricane's winds are very strong. But in its center, or eye, the air is calm. Some birds, such as pelicans and seagulls, fly into the eye of a hurricane to escape the wind. However, they must be able to fly with the storm as it moves.

Each animal's escape response is different. It depends on its body type and where it lives. But when in danger, many animals flee on land, in the air, or through the water to survive.

Explore Online

Visit the website below. Does it give any new information about flying animals that wasn't in Chapter Four?

Flying Squirrel

abdocorelibrary.com/fleeing-to -survive

SURVIVAL FACTS

Some animals use speed to flee from predators or other dangers.

Animals can sometimes avoid danger by quickly changing directions.

Some land animals can use water to escape danger.

Flying squirrels, snakes, and frogs can flee through the air.

Glossary

burrows
tunnels or holes in the ground that are home to some animals

camouflage
a color or shape that protects an animal from attack by making it difficult to see in its surroundings

escape response
how an animal reacts to and avoids danger

jink
to move quickly or unexpectedly with sudden turns and shifts

membrane
a flexible, thin layer of skin or tissue

schools
groups of fish or other sea creatures

Online Resources

To learn more about fleeing to survive, visit our free resource websites below.

Visit **abdocorelibrary.com** or scan this QR code for free Common Core resources for teachers and students, including vetted activities, multimedia, and booklinks, for deeper subject comprehension.

Visit **abdobooklinks.com** or scan this QR code for free additional online weblinks for further learning. These links are routinely monitored and updated to provide the most current information available.

Learn More

Huddleston, Emma. *How Mammals Run*. Abdo, 2021.

Jenkins, Steve, and Robin Page. *The Frog Book*. Houghton Mifflin Harcourt, 2019.

Index

About the Author

Laura Perdew is a mom, writing consultant, and author of more than 40 books for children. She writes both fiction and nonfiction with a focus on nature, the environment, and environmental issues. She lives and plays in Boulder, Colorado.